D006259

JUN 09

CHECKERBOARD HOW-TO LIBRARY

COOL CRAFTS

Cool Melt & Pour Soap

Lisa Wagner

ABDO
Publishing Company

visit us at
www.abdopub.com

Published by ABDO Publishing Company, 4940 Viking Drive, Edina, Minnesota 55435. Copyright © 2005 by Abdo Consulting Group, Inc. International copyrights reserved in all countries. No part of this book may be reproduced in any form without written permission from the publisher. Checkerboard Library is a trademark and logo of ABDO Publishing Company.

Printed in the United States.

Design and Production: Mighty Media, Inc.
    Cover Photo: Anders Hanson
    Interior Photos: Kelly Doudna
    Series Coordinator: Pam Scheunemann
    Editor: Pam Price
    Art Direction: Pam Scheunemann

Library of Congress Cataloging-in-Publication Data

Wagner, Lisa, 1958-
    Cool melt & pour soaps / Lisa Wagner.
      p. cm. -- (Cool crafts)
    Includes index.
    ISBN 1-59197-741-X
    1. Soap--Juvenile literature. I. Title. II. Series.

TT991.W24 2005
668'.12--dc22

2004046291

For Your Safety

Soap base is heated to about 140 degrees (60°C). Serious burns can occur if hot, melted soap base contacts skin. For your safety, always have an adult help with soap-making projects. In addition, some of the tools shown in this book should be used only when an adult is present.

Contents

Boldfaced words throughout the text are defined in the glossary.

Introduction

Welcome to the ancient world of soap making! Soap was discovered more than 4,000 years ago in Greece. The first soap was made by nature, not by people. People just noticed it, and then they copied the natural process to make their own soap.

It happened like this. Melted fat and ashes from animal sacrifices washed down Mount Sapo in the rain. The mixture flowed into the clay soil on the banks of the Tiber River. The women washing clothes in the river noticed something unusual. Their clothes got cleaner, and with less effort! Our modern word *soap* comes from Mount Sapo.

People were happy to discover the benefits of soap, and they started making their own. For many years, making soap was a household chore.

When factories began to make soap in huge batches, people didn't have to make their own anymore. Handmade soaps became luxury items. Luckily, luxurious soap doesn't have to cost a fortune when you make your own. That's what this book is all about.

You'll learn everything you need to make your own soap. The materials are simple and inexpensive, and the melt-and-pour process is easy. Use your own creativity with shape, color, and **fragrance**, and the possibilities are endless.

Basic Supplies

You probably already have many of the supplies you need to make melt-and-pour soap. For the melt part, you need a source of heat. A microwave oven is ideal for melting the soap base. We'll be using one to make the projects in this book. You need microwave-safe glass or plastic containers for melting the base.

You can also use the stovetop and melt the base in a double boiler. If you don't have a double boiler, you can improvise. Set a heat-resistant glass measuring cup or a small pan in a pan partially filled with boiling water. Use heat-resistant glass or metal containers if you are using the improvised double boiler.

Glass measuring cups usually have a little pouring lip. That makes it easier to pour the soap into the molds. Your mixing stick can be a chopstick, spoon, or glass rod made especially for stirring.

Cut the soap base on an acrylic cutting board. Try to have one that's just used for soap making. It's hard to clean any cutting board perfectly, and you don't want your food to taste like soap!

You can use a knife or a cheese slicer to cut the base into small pieces. You also need a knife to trim rough edges off soap or to slice loaf soap.

For adding **fragrance** and color, use a glass eyedropper. Make sure it's glass. Plastic won't work because some fragrances can melt plastic. Plus, it's hard to clean. Many colors and fragrances come in bottles that already have dropper tops.

Small measuring spoons can be used for measuring fragrance oils. An eighth or quarter teaspoon ($\frac{2}{3}$ to 1½ ml) will work fine. Don't use these for measuring food products once they have been used for soap making.

Use a pump spray bottle to spray the soaps with rubbing alcohol. This helps to get rid of bubbles on the soap surface. Also, spraying between pours in a layered soap will help one layer stick to the next.

Waxed paper works well for protecting your work surface. You can also use newspaper or an old plastic tablecloth.

Cookie sheets are helpful for moving around batches of molds or trays.

Clear plastic wrap works well for wrapping finished soaps. Stretch it tight across the soaps and seal the edges carefully. It gives the soap a professional look and it protects the soap from air. If a melt-and-pour soap is left unwrapped, it can sweat. Drops of moisture appear on the surface of the soap and spoil the look.

Important!

Always get an adult to supervise when you're using a microwave, stovetop, or sharp knife.

Soap Bases & Molds

All of the soap projects in this book use a glycerin base. Glycerin soap base is also called melt-and-pour soap base. Glycerin is a thick liquid that can be vegetable-based or **synthetic**. The synthetic base is created from a petroleum **by-product**. The natural base gives the best finished product, and it's better for your skin too.

Glycerin soap base melts at a fairly low temperature and turns into a clear liquid. Once the liquid is poured into a mold, it hardens in about an hour.

Most of the projects in this book use clear glycerin soap base. Some projects also use **opaque** glycerin soap base that has a mineral added to whiten it. You can also buy glycerin soap base that contains goat's milk, coconut oil, olive oil, or avocado. These added ingredients make the soap moist and add moisture to your skin.

Glycerin soap base is sold by the pound or kilogram in various amounts. The price per pound goes down when you buy larger quantities. A five-pound (2 kg) block is a good starter amount. You can make four or more bars of soap from each pound of soap base. Most soap molds make either three- or four-ounce (100 g) bars of soap.

Molds

Molds really make the soaps! You'll be surprised at how easily a mold can make your soap look professional. Most of the projects in this book use purchased molds, but we will make one too.

A mold can be a simple item you have at home. Plastic containers, cardboard juice cans, and pieces of **PVC** pipe make great molds. Glass, wood, and sturdy metal don't work well. The most important thing about a found or homemade mold is to choose something flexible. You want your soap to pop right out of a mold.

Be sure to choose a mold that can take a little heat. The melted soap base is about 140 degrees (60°C) when you pour it into a mold. A flimsy container might melt or lose its shape when the hot soap base is poured into it.

Individual molds and tray molds come in a variety of shapes and designs. Loaf molds let you make a large batch of soap and cut it into several individual bars. There are molds for holidays, seasons, and special occasions. You can find molds shaped like seashells, animals, flowers, hearts, stars, and just about anything else.

Since soap making is becoming so popular, new molds are available all the time. You can buy molds at craft or candy supply stores. You can also order them by mail or online.

Fragrance & Color

First you look at a soap, then you smell it. A soap with a wonderful **fragrance** is a treasure. It's fun to experiment with fragrances and create unique blends. You can get fragrances that are made especially for soaps. These will be **cosmetic** grade, which means they will not be harmful to your skin.

Some people have really sensitive skin. They might prefer soaps made without fragrance or even color. If your soap will be a gift, find out if the person prefers soaps without fragrance or color.

Fragrance

Essential oils and fragrance oils can be added to melted soap base. You can use both essential oil and fragrance oil in the same batch of soap.

Essential oils are highly concentrated and are made from natural plant and flower ingredients. You only have to use a couple of drops to get a pleasing scent. Essential oils have names like vanilla or lavender. They are usually more expensive than fragrance oils. You can buy essential oils at most natural food stores.

Fragrance oils are **synthetic** and less expensive and less concentrated than essential oils. Since they are less concentrated, it takes more than a couple of drops to get a nice scent. Fragrance oils are often blends of oils with names like Ocean

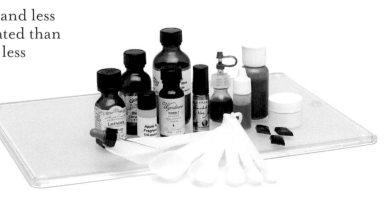

or Rain Forest. You can get **fragrance** oils at craft supply stores or order them from suppliers online.

Color

Color and fragrance work together to make soap beautiful and unique. A pretty yellow soap is perfect with a fresh lemon scent. Ocean scent is a wonderful choice for a blue seashell-shaped soap. A red-and-white layered soap with a peppermint scent makes a festive holiday gift. It's fun to experiment with combinations of color and fragrance.

Most of the projects in this book use a liquid-based color product. Liquid color comes in great colors and mixes easily with the soap base. You can also use powdered color additives, color shavings, and colored chips.

Color additives are concentrated, so go slow. Add just a little at a time and mix it carefully into the melted base. You can always add more for a deeper color but you can't take it out.

Always use color additives that are made especially for soap-making projects. Food coloring is not a good choice for tinting soaps. It doesn't mix well with the soap base, the color isn't rich, and it can stain your skin. Be sure to use a **cosmetic-**grade color additive to avoid skin irritation.

You can get color additives at craft supply stores or order them from suppliers online.

Basic Techniques

All of the projects in this book use the techniques shown on the following pages. We will go into detail here to give you a good understanding of the process. Most projects will refer you back to this section of the book.

Each project will tell you which colors and **fragrances** to use. Or, you can use the supplies you have on hand instead. Use your imagination and make your own combinations of color and fragrance! For the basic instructions about using color and fragrance, read this section carefully.

Keep It Safe

Keep soap-making supplies, especially fragrance oils and knives, out of the reach of small children.

Have an adult supervise if you are using a microwave oven, stovetop, or knife.

Melted soap base and the containers used to melt it can get hot. Be very careful when handling melted soap base because it can burn your skin.

Essential oils and fragrance oils should never be used right on your skin. They are concentrated and need to be blended with soap base so they won't irritate your skin.

Essential oils are poisonous if taken internally. Never put them in your mouth!

Protect your work surface with waxed paper, newspaper, or an old tablecloth. Some oils can be harmful to wood surfaces.

Wipe up spills right away. If soap base spills on the floor, it can get slippery. You don't want anyone to fall, and you don't want to slip with a beautiful tray of soap!

1 Select the colors and **fragrance** oils you will use. Think about the mold you are using and choose your color and fragrance. Set the color and fragrance oils on your work surface within easy reach.

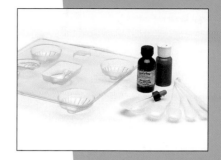

2 Fill the mold with water, then pour the water into a measuring cup. This will show you about how much melted soap base you will need to fill the mold. Then carefully dry the mold and set it on your work surface.

3 Cut the soap base into small chunks. Small pieces will melt faster than large pieces. Make the pieces about the same size so they will melt evenly. Some soap base will stick to the container when you pour it out, so always melt a little extra.

4 Put the chopped-up soap base in a microwave-safe, heat-resistant container. A glass measuring cup works well for this.

5 Place the container in the microwave oven or over a double boiler. We used a microwave oven to melt the soap base for all the projects in this book.

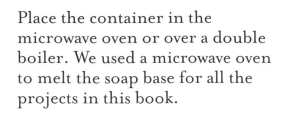

6 You want the soap base to melt, but you don't want it to boil. Start by using high power for 30 seconds. If you are making several bars of soap at once, it will take longer to melt the base. You can start with 60 seconds for larger batches.

7 Remove the container and stir the soap gently. Don't stir too much, though. That will make air bubbles in the soap. If it hasn't melted completely, return the soap base to the microwave for 30 seconds more on high power.

8 Keep going in 30-second rounds until the soap base is completely melted. Remember to stir gently each time you remove the soap base from the microwave.

9 When the soap base is melted, add the color a little at a time. You can always add more to make the color richer. Stir gently to keep air bubbles to a minimum.

10 Add **fragrance** when the soap base has cooled a bit. Fragrance oils will lose their scent if they are poured into hot soap base. Add a little at a time, but work quickly so the soap base doesn't harden.

11 Carefully pour the melted soap base into the mold. Try to pour just to the top of the mold but not over it.

12 It is common to find a few bubbles on top of the soap. Remove these by spraying alcohol on the surface.

13 The soap will begin to harden right away. You can put the mold in the refrigerator if you want to speed up the process. However, letting soap harden overnight is best, if you can stand to wait that long!

14 When the soap is hardened, flex the mold to pop out the soap. If the soap doesn't come out easily, let it harden some more. Try not to handle the soap too much. It looks better without fingerprints on it.

15 Stretch a piece of clear plastic wrap tightly around the soap. With a little practice, you can do this without making fingerprints on the soap. If there is extra wrap, trim it off.

16 You can also slip the finished soap into a cellophane bag. Seal it with a twist tie or a piece of ribbon.

Clean-up Time

Wash all your molds and utensils by hand and dry them carefully. Don't put containers or molds in the dishwasher. The soap base will make way too many bubbles and a big mess! Keep the items you use for soap making separate from utensils and containers you use for food.

Replace the caps on all color and **fragrance** bottles. Wrap leftover soap base in airtight packaging to protect it from moisture.

Get It in Writing

Keep a soap recipe notebook. Make notes about the molds, fragrances, and colors you use as you work. Before long, you'll have your own collection of soap recipes!

Blend fragrance oils in a paper cup before adding them to the melted soap base. Experiment with different blends of fragrance. Be sure to keep notes about your favorites so you can make the blends again.

Layered Soaps

Layered soaps are some of the prettiest soaps you can make. Layer colors and **fragrances** in a loaf mold or in individual molds.

What You Need

- ‣ Heart-shaped mold
- ‣ Clear soap base
- ‣ Opaque soap base
- ‣ Red liquid color
- ‣ Pink liquid color
- ‣ Rose fragrance
- ‣ Ylang-ylang essential oil
- ‣ Spray bottle with alcohol

1 Follow the instructions on page 13 to estimate how much soap base to melt. You will need two layers of clear and one layer of **opaque**. Cut the soap base and put it into separate containers for melting.

2 Follow the instructions on page 14 for melting the soap base. You will make the layers one at a time. Melt only the base you need for the layer you are working on. Have your **fragrance**, color, and supplies handy.

3 For the first layer, add pink color a drop at a time to the clear melted base. If you don't have pink, use a tiny bit of red. When you get a color you like, add rose fragrance until you are happy with the scent.

4 Fill the heart-shaped molds about one-third full. Just before you add the next layer, spray this layer with alcohol.

5 Melt the **opaque** soap base. This layer will be white, so don't add any color to it. Add the ylang-ylang **essential oil** a drop at a time and mix gently. The soap already in the mold should be firm but not hard at this point.

6 Check to see that the second layer is firm, then spray it with alcohol.

7 The final layer is red. Melt the clear base and add red color a drop at a time. Add the rose **fragrance** and stir gently to mix. Pour this last layer into the mold, filling it to the top.

8 Let the soap harden. Then unmold it and wrap it in clear plastic wrap or put it in a cellophane bag and close it with a twist tie.

More Ideas for Layered Soaps

You can make layered soaps in any combination of colors and **fragrances** that pleases you. When using more than one fragrance in a soap, be sure to open both bottles and check what the fragrances smell like together. Not all fragrances work well together.

Choose a mold that complements the theme of the soap or use what you have on hand. For example, we made the Citrus Sunshine soap in a rectangular mold. But, a sun-shaped mold would be nice too.

Earth and Sky

Earth and Sky soap features soothing tones of green and blue. The blue layer is scented with Ocean fragrance. The green layer is scented with Fresh Spring fragrance.

Use clear soap base for both layers. Make the soap in a loaf mold and slice it into bars after the soap has hardened.

Citrus Sunshine

Make Citrus Sunshine soap in warm, sunny shades of yellow, orange, and green separated by **opaque** white. Scent the clear colored layers with lemon, orange, and lime **essential oils**. Be sure to choose a mold deep enough to accommodate all five layers.

Treasure Soaps

Treasure soaps make wonderful gifts! You're really giving two gifts at once. There's a soap to use now and a treasure to keep when the soap is gone. Our Creepy Insects soaps hold some creepy surprises inside! The amber color of the soaps makes them look almost like fossils in resin.

What You Need

- Deep rectangular mold
- Plastic insect that fits in the mold
- Clear soap base
- Orange liquid color
- Yellow liquid color
- Woods fragrance
- Spray bottle with alcohol

1 Follow the instructions on page 13 to estimate how much soap base to melt. Follow the instructions on page 14 for melting the soap base. Have your **fragrance**, color, treasures, and supplies handy.

2 Add a drop of orange and a drop of yellow color. Gently stir to blend. Then adjust the color by adding more of either one. Mix in the Woods fragrance.

3 Pour the melted soap base into the mold to a depth of about a quarter inch (7 mm). When there is a layer of skin on top, gently remove it with a knife. Now the soap is at the right temperature for embedding the plastic insects.

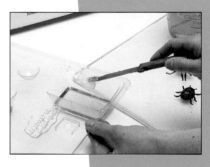

4 This first layer is called the holding layer because it holds the treasure in place. Spray the insects with alcohol before putting them in the holding layer.

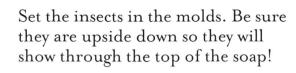

Set the insects in the molds. Be sure they are upside down so they will show through the top of the soap!

When the holding layer is firm, remelt the rest of the soap base. Spray the holding layer and the insect with alcohol. Fill the mold to the top and spray away the air bubbles on top with alcohol.

Let the soap harden. Then unmold it and wrap it in clear plastic wrap or a cellophane bag with a twist tie.

More Ideas for Treasure Soaps

Treasure soaps make very personal gifts. That's because you can choose a treasure that reflects the interests of the person you give the soap to. Here are two more treasure soaps that are very different from the Creepy Insects soap shown on the previous pages.

Goldfish in a Pond

For this soap, rubber goldfish are embedded in clear soap base scented with Rainwater fragrance. To make it look like a fish you just bought at the pet shop, make this soap right in a cellophane bag!

To make Goldfish in a Pond, melt clear soap base and stir in Rainwater **fragrance**. Put a cellophane bag in a mug to help it hold its shape. Pour a layer of clear base into the bag.

Spray the goldfish with alcohol, then set it into this holding layer. When the holding layer is set, spray the holding layer and the goldfish with alcohol. Then fill the bag about one-third full with the rest of the clear base. Once the soap hardens, close the bag with a twist tie.

Luxurious Jeweled Soaps

These super-elegant soaps have sparkly plastic jewels inside. The lightly tinted clear soap base is scented with patchouli **essential oil**.

To make Luxurious Jeweled Soaps, pour the holding layer into a deep mold. Spray a large plastic jewel with alcohol and set it into the holding layer. Spray the holding layer and the jewel with alcohol and pour in the remaining melted soap base.

Loofah Soaps

It's a soap and washcloth all in one! It's a natural **loofah** sponge embedded in a bed of soap. We colored clear soap base with violet and scented it with relaxing lavender **essential oil**. But let your imagination be your guide to choosing colors and **fragrances**. Forest fragrance in green-tinted clear soap base makes for an enchanting bath treat. Or try refreshing citrus fragrance and bright yellow color.

What You Need

- 3½-inch (9-cm) diameter PVC pipe cut to a 4-inch (10-cm) length. (You can buy this at a hardware store and they will cut it for you.)
- Loofah sponge cut in 1½- to 2-inch (4- to 5-cm) sections
- Clear soap base
- Violet liquid color
- Lavender essential oil
- Aluminum foil
- Rubber bands
- Vegetable spray

1
To make your mold, cover one end of the **PVC** pipe with aluminum foil. Hold the foil in place with rubber bands. Coat the inside with vegetable oil spray. Wipe off any excess oil.

2
Stand the **loofah** section inside the mold. Follow the steps on pages 13 and 14 to cut, measure, and melt the soap base. Add drops of violet color until you have a shade you like. Mix in lavender **essential oil**.

3
Pour the melted soap base into the mold up to the top of the loofah sponge. Let the soap harden overnight.

4
Remove the aluminum foil and push the finished soap out of the mold. Package it in clear plastic wrap or a cellophane bag tied with a ribbon.

Relief Soaps

Any soap mold with a raised **motif** has exciting creative possibilities. Mix and match clear and **opaque** soap bases with color in a simple two-step process.

What You Need

- Mold with relief motif
- Opaque soap base
- Dark green liquid color
- Blue liquid color
- Cedar essential oil
- Sandalwood essential oil
- Spray bottle with alcohol

1 Start by melting just enough soap base to fill only the **relief** design in the mold. Cut the soap base and put it into a container for melting. Have your **fragrance**, color, and supplies handy.

2 Melt the soap base. Add a couple drops of dark green color. Stir gently to blend, then add more color if needed. Mix in the cedar essential oil. Pour carefully to fill only the relief design in the mold.

3 While the relief layer hardens, melt the rest of the soap base. Add a few drops of blue color until you like the way it looks. Add sandalwood **essential oil** and mix gently. Spray the relief layer with alcohol.

4 Fill the mold to the top and spray away the air bubbles on top with alcohol. Let the soap harden. Then unmold it and wrap it in clear plastic wrap or a cellophane bag with a twist tie.

More Ideas for Relief Soaps

Ideas for **relief** soaps are limited only by your imagination! There are many different molds available. Choose any colors and **fragrances** you like. Here are two more relief soaps to get you started.

Fleur-de-lis soap

The classic **fleur-de-lis motif** makes this soap simply elegant. It features bergamot **essential oil** and uses both clear and **opaque** soap base. The relief is made with rose-tinted clear soap base. The main part of the soap is opaque soap base without added color.

Celtic relief soap

Make this luxurious soap with opaque soap base, shades of turquoise blue, and Fresh Spring fragrance. Because you will use shades of only one color, you can melt all the base in one container. Lightly tint the soap base and pour only the relief layer. Then add more color to the rest of soap base and pour the final layer.

Glossary

by-product - an additional product produced while making the intended product.

cosmetic - of or relating to beauty, especially in regard to skin. Products that are cosmetic grade are appropriate for use on skin.

essential oil - oil that gives a plant its odor. Essential oils are extracted from flowers or leaves for use in perfumes and flavorings.

fleur-de-lis - a three-petaled iris used as an emblem on the armor of the kings of France.

fragrance - a substance designed to give off a pleasing scent.

loofah - a tropical vine with a long, cylindrical fruit. A loofah sponge is the dried, fibrous inside of a loofah fruit.

motif - a design in architecture or decoration that is usually repeated but sometimes single.

opaque - blocking the passage of light.

PVC - abbreviation for polyvinyl chloride, a type of plastic.

relief - having shapes that are raised above the surrounding surface.

synthetic - manufactured rather than found in nature.

Web Sites

To learn more about soap making, visit ABDO Publishing Company on the World Wide Web at **www.abdopub.com**. Web sites about soap making are featured on our Book Links page. These links are routinely monitored and updated to provide the most current information available.

Index